PLANET EARTH

COASTLINES

Sheila Padget

Chapter II

The Bookwright Press
New York · 1984

PLANET EARTH

Coastlines
Volcanoes
The Oceans
Water on the Land
The Work of the Wind
Weather and Climate

First published in the United States in 1984 by
The Bookwright Press, 387 Park Avenue South,
New York, NY 10016

First published in 1983 by
Wayland (Publishers) Ltd
49 Lansdowne Place, Hove
East Sussex BN3 1HF, England

ISBN 0-531-04792-X

Library of Congress Catalog Card Number 83-72794

Printed in Italy by
G. Canale & C.S.p.A., Turin

Contents

Vacationers relaxing on a sandy Spanish beach. Have you ever wondered how beaches and other coastal features were formed?

At the edge of the land

The coastline is where the land meets the sea. It is a place of enormous variety and great fascination. Sometimes the pounding of the waves wears away the land to produce steep cliffs; elsewhere the land merges gently into the sea in the form of a beach. In some places the coastline is almost straight for long stretches; in other places it is a series of tiny bays and jutting headlands.

For hundreds of years, people have made a living from the sea, either by fishing or by trading with other countries. Because of this, many towns and cities have developed in coastal areas.

In recent times, many more people have been attracted to the coast for their vacations. Have you ever spent a vacation by the ocean? Did you ever stop to wonder where the sand or pebbles on the beach came from, why there are cliffs, or how caves are made?

This book will tell you about these and other coastal features, and explain how the coastline is shaped by the never-ending battle between the sea and the land.

A spectacular line of chalk cliffs—the Seven Sisters, on the coast of Sussex, England.

The sea erodes the land

The shape of any coastline changes constantly as the sea removes material from one stretch of coast and deposits it elsewhere. Usually, the changes happen so slowly that they are not noticeable. However, after a violent storm some changes may be easy to see.

Waves and tides

Wave action is one of the most important factors in bringing about changes in the coastline. Waves are caused by wind

The circular movement of water droplets in waves, caused by wind blowing across the sea.

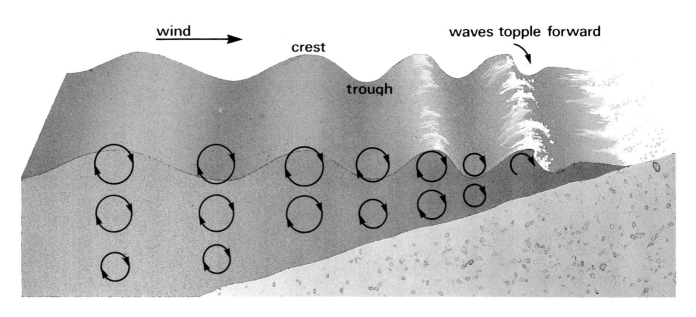

wind → crest

waves topple forward

trough

blowing over open water. As the wind blows, it causes the surface of the water to ripple. The droplets of water do not move forward with the wind; they travel round in a circle, as shown in the diagram. The top of the circle is the **crest** of the wave and the bottom is the **trough**. It is the positions of these crests and troughs that move forward with the wind.

When waves reach the shore, their circular movement is broken by the upward slope of the sea floor. The waves

Storm waves approaching the coast.
Waves like these can be very destructive.

then topple forward, their tops breaking into white foam as they plunge onto the shore.

The height and length of the waves depend upon the strength of the wind and the **fetch** (the distance over which the waves have built up). Storm waves are high, and short from crest to crest. They travel fast and are very destructive. Waves that are long from crest to crest, and short from crest to trough are constructive.

Tides are caused by the sun and moon pulling on the Earth and causing "bulges" in the oceans.

Tsunamis are the most destructive waves of all. They are caused by under water earthquakes or volcanic eruptions and can travel across an ocean at 500-800 kilometers per hour (300-500 miles per

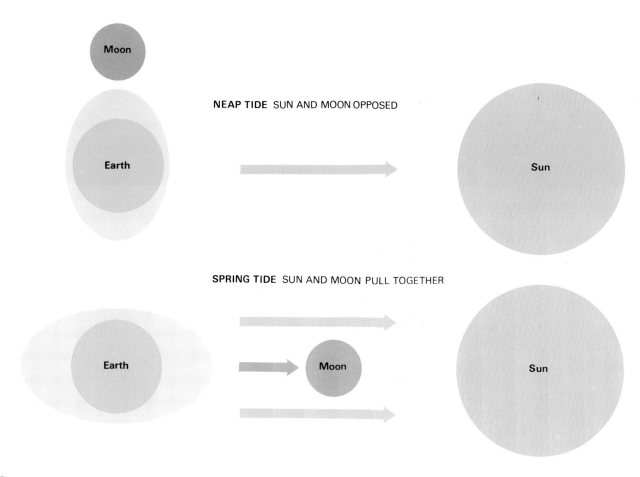

NEAP TIDE SUN AND MOON OPPOSED

SPRING TIDE SUN AND MOON PULL TOGETHER

hour). When Krakatoa exploded in 1883, a wall of water 35 meters (115 feet) high swept across Java and Sumatra, killing 36,000 people.

Tides change the height at which waves attack the coast. They are caused by the moon and sun pulling on the Earth and causing "bulges" in the oceans. There are usually two high and two low tides in every 24 hours. Each high tide occurs 12 hours 25 minutes after the previous one.

Powerful storm waves can break up massive stone sea defenses.

In some narrow estuaries, such as the Bay of Fundy in Nova Scotia, Canada, the difference between the levels of high and low tide can be 12 meters (40 feet) or more.

Besides waves and tides, ocean currents are important in transporting material along the coast.

The work of the waves

The destructive power of storm waves is not hard to imagine. The pressure of the water being hurled against the coast during the winter storm is enormous, and it is not surprising under such conditions that waves have been known to break up and move massive stone breakwaters and sea defenses. But how do waves erode or wear away a coast during normal conditions?

Waves attack the coast in three ways.

Hydraulic action No cliff-face is perfectly flat and smooth. There are always cracks and crevices. Each time a wave hits the cliff-face, the air trapped in the cracks is squashed or compressed. The increased pressure acts like a wedge being driven into the rock, forcing it apart. As the wave falls away, the pressure is suddenly released again, putting even more strain on the rock. Continual changes in air pressure weaken the rocks and eventually break off pieces.

The action of the sea has worn a notch at the base of this cliff, and a cave may eventually develop.

Corrasive action Waves breaking against a cliff-face usually carry shingle and pebbles that help to wear away and break off pieces of the cliff. Even sand constantly swirling against the foot of the cliff acts like a giant file. Most corrasive action takes place at the base of the cliff, although boulders and pebbles may be hurled higher up the face by very rough seas. In time a notch is worn at the base of the cliff. The overhanging cliff face is eventually weakened and will collapse

Very soft rocks, like these siltstones on the coast of Iran, are easily eroded by the sea.

onto the beach. This provides more material for the waves to pick up.

You may have noticed that most beach pebbles have smooth, well-rounded edges. As pebbles and boulders are rolled around by the sea, they are rubbed against one another and are themselves worn away. This process is called attrition.

Solvent action Sea water contains dissolved chemicals that make it slightly acidic. Rocks such as chalk and limestone are easily dissolved by acidic water. Where the cliffs are formed of such rocks, waves and spray penetrate any cracks or joints and dissolve away the rock to make deep, narrow clefts in the cliffs.

Hard rocks and soft rocks

Waves and tides erode the coast. How fast the erosion takes place depends upon the structure and hardness of the coastal rocks. Most old rocks are hard and tough, and take a long time to be worn away. Younger rocks are usually softer and more crumbly, and are easily worn away. Rocks that have few cracks or joints are also able to resist erosion.

Many rocks have well-developed horizontal joints called **bedding planes**. Sometimes, powerful earth movements tilt the rocks, causing their bedding planes to lie at an angle, and this can produce different cliff shapes. If the rocks slope down toward the sea, landslips can occur as pieces of rock slide down the bedding planes. But if the rocks tilt inland, then a more stable stepped cliff is produced.

It is impossible to say generally how fast coastal erosion takes place. The rate varies for each section of coastline. Although the west coast of Britain is open to attack by powerful waves from the Atlantic Ocean, most of the rocks are very resistant, and the rate of erosion is slow.

The part of the British Isles where erosion is taking place the fastest is Holderness. Holderness is that part of the Yorkshire coast between Flamborough Head and Spurn Point. The coast here is made up of soft clays that are being worn away at a rate of 2 meters (6.5 feet) a year. Studies of old maps show many villages and towns that have now disappeared beneath the sea.

Many stretches of coast are composed of rocks of varying resistance, which results in the formation of particular types of coastlines. In many areas of hilly coastline, both bands of soft rock and hills lie at right angles to the coastline. The bands of soft rock tend to get worn away

Opposite *Although the west coast of Britain is pounded by powerful waves from the Atlantic, erosion is slow because the rocks are very hard.*

more quickly than the harder rocks, producing a series of bays and headlands.

In contrast, along other kinds of coastline, both the bands of rock and the line of hills lie parallel to the coast. Here, bands of limestone, clays and sands may once have been continuous. But waves attack points of weakness in the limestone and eventually break through to make small coves. Once the limestone is breached and the waves are able to attack the softer clays and sands beyond, then erosion is far more rapid. However, if the waves reach a more resistant rock behind, erosion is once again slowed

Lulworth Cove on the south Dorset coast of England.

down. The shape of Lulworth Cove, in England, shows this very clearly.

A coast is worn away

Many of the most interesting features of coastal erosion occur during cliff formation. When waves attack a cliff-face, they pick out any lines of weakness, such as joints or bedding planes in the rock. A notch is cut in the cliff-face at the point where the waves attack most strongly, and this gradually becomes larger. After a time, the weakened cliff-face above the notch crumbles and collapses. This process of crumble and collapse occurs again and again, and slowly the cliff-face is worn back. A rocky shelf or platform called a **bench** is left at the base of the cliff. The waves then have to travel across the platform before they reach the cliff.

The wave-cut bench may become covered with beach deposits. Further collapses of the cliff-face will drop rubble onto this platform. The waves sort all the material and grade it according to size—you have probably noticed how some beaches vary from coarse pebbles near the cliff to fine sand exposed at low tide. The

A wave-cut bench on the southwest coast of France. Notice that the rocks have been tilted and the bedding planes dip down toward the sea.

constant rolling and grinding of the beach deposits over the wave-cut bench helps to erode the platform itself. For this reaᵣon, bench platforms slope gently toward the sea. The outer part has been scoured and eroded longer than the area closer to the cliff-face.

As the wave-cut bench becomes wider, it eventually slows down the process of cliff formation. The waves have so far to travel across the platform that they lose their energy before reaching the cliff. The cliff then becomes stable. Some wave-cut benches are very wide—one of the most spectacular is the *Strandflat* of northwest Norway, which is 45 kilometers (28 miles) wide in places.

Sometimes during the process of cliff formation, waves attack some joints more strongly than others. When this happens, a definite hole forms in the rock. This hole is enlarged by hydraulic action to produce a cave. Waves continue to break inside the cave and enlarge it still further, and the roof often becomes weakened and may collapse. The collapse will occur slowly. At first, a hole or chimney forms, leading up to the clifftop; this is called a **blowhole**. In rough weather, waves breaking inside the cave can throw spray up through the blowhole. On the coast of the Faroe Islands, there are a number of long,

As waves break in the cave below, spray is thrown up through this blowhole on the clifftop.

The sea has cut through these rocks to form arches and stacks.

narrow inlets running inland from the cliff-face. These inlets, called **geos**, probably developed from collapsed caves.

If two caves form on opposite sides of a headland, in time their back walls may break through to make a natural **arch**. The roof of the arch will eventually weaken and collapse also, leaving isolated pillars of rock, called **stacks**, standing separate from the cliff-face. Gradually the stacks will be completely eroded away. Like arches and caves, they are only temporary features produced during cliff formation.

Moving eroded rocks

The debris produced by coastal erosion, and the material dropped in the sea by rivers, is moved or **transported** by waves and currents. Heavy boulders and pebbles are rolled along the seabed. Lighter particles move by a series of jerks and jumps known as **saltation**. The smallest particles are carried in suspension. All the time it is moving, the debris is constantly being ground down and sorted according to size.

Each time a wave breaks on the shore, the water travels up the beach as the **swash** and then retreats down the slope of the

Longshore drift: the wind blows waves up the beach at an angle, and they then return down the steepest slope, so the material carried by the waves is moved along the coast from left to right.

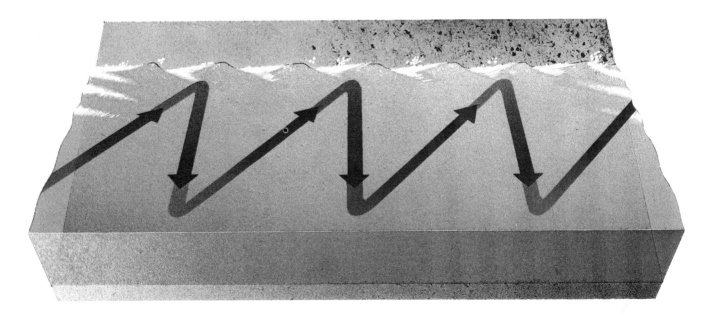

beach as the **backwash**. It is the swash and backwash that move material up and down a beach.

Most waves approach the shore at an angle. So the swash moves up the beach at an angle but the backwash returns directly down the steepest slope. In this way material is moved along the beach in a zig-zag manner as shown in the diagram. This is called **longshore drift**. Longshore drifting is very common along the coast of southern England, where material is moved from west to east. In many places

Groins help to reduce longshore drift and preserve the beach.

groins have been built across the beach to halt the movement of beach material.

Waves also disturb and churn up large amounts of fine material from the sea bed. Some is transported along the coast by longshore currents and may help to build up ridges in the sea. The undertow, the movement of water away from the coast along the sea floor, also carries large amounts of fine material out to sea.

New land from the sea

The material carried by waves and currents will be transported until some obstacle slows the movement of the water. Then the material will be dropped or deposited. Headlands, which project into the sea, have this effect. Rivers flowing into the sea also slow the movement of sea water, as do winds and currents moving against the main flow.

Deposition, like erosion, is a slow process. The way in which material is deposited is also irregular, as the power of the waves and currents varies. Some deposition occurs along the coast, some offshore. Wherever it takes place, deposition helps to build up new land.

Beaches

The most obvious feature of deposition is the **beach**. The beach is the part of the shore that lies between the low water mark and the highest point reached by storm waves. Beach deposits vary in size from small boulders to fine sand.

In general, resistant cliffed coasts have only a narrow fringe of beach. But lowland coasts often have a wide expanse of sand. Where there are a series of headlands and bays, it is the bays that have well-developed bayhead beaches. As the waves approach the shore, they spread

Beaches are formed when the material being carried by the waves and currents is dropped.

20

out in the bays. This slows them down and they deposit the material they are carrying at the bayhead.

Some beaches have ridges of coarser deposits lying parallel to the coast. These are built up by constructive waves, which are long from crest to crest but short from crest to trough. They follow one another slowly to the coast. These waves break gently on to the beach and most of their energy is put into the swash. The back wash from one wave returns before the next wave breaks. So these waves move material up the beach and build up beach ridges.

Where a beach is made up of a wide expanse of sand, strong winds blowing on shore may pile up the sand to form **coastal dunes**. The wind can blow the dunes inland over valuable farmland. So dunes are usually planted with marram grass with long spreading roots. The roots help to hold the sand together and stop the dunes from being moved any farther.

Ridges in the sea

Bars are ridges of sand or **shingle** (coarse gravels) that build up parallel to the coast. They form on gently sloping shores and

These dunes on the coast of France are being driven inland by the wind.

often grow across the mouths of rivers.

The circular movement of the waves stirs up the seabed and erodes any loose material. Because of the gentle slope, the waves break out at sea. The material they are carrying is deposited and a bar is slowly built up. It will start below the surface as a submarine bar but may eventually be built up above sea level.

Some bars grow from one headland to another and are called **bayhead bars**. The Looe bar in Cornwall, England, is an example. Much of the material in the Looe bar has come from erosion of the cliffs to the west. It has been carried eastward by longshore drift. In the Cape Hatteras area on the coast of North Carolina, there are some huge bars with large **lagoons** behind them. The famous beaches of Daytona, Palm Beach and Miami, in Florida, are offshore bars, too.

Bars that grow offshore slowly move inland. Waves move the sand or shingle from outside the bar, over the top, and deposit it again on the innerside. In time

Above *Beach ripples at low tide.*

Opposite *The beach at Miami, Florida, is really an offshore bar with a lagoon behind it.*

the bay or lagoon behind the bar may silt up. Fine deposits are carried into the lagoon by the waves, or blown in by the wind. Any rivers entering the lagoon from the land will also deposit all the material they are carrying. This builds up slowly until it rises above sea level. Then salt-loving plants begin to grow and trap more silt. In this way, large areas of salt marsh develop.

Most bars are formed offshore, but **spits** are ridges of sand or shingle that are attached to the coast at one end. Spits grow from the coast and are built up by longshore drift and not by material eroded from the seabed. A spit will keep growing until it reaches water too deep to allow the sand or shingle to build up. Some spits grow parallel to the coast; others grow at an angle.

Some of the best-known examples of spits occur around Gdansk, on the Baltic coast of Poland. Here the spits, called *nehrungs*, grow across river estuaries and bays in the coast to enclose lagoons called *haffs*.

Chesil Beach, in England, is a special

A sand spit on the coast of Dorset, England.

type of spit called a **tombolo**. Tombolos are spits that link an island to the main land. Chesil Beach is a shingle ridge 26 kilometers (16 miles) long, linking the Dorset coast to the Isle of Portland. It will not grow any longer because the long shore drift is stopped by the Isle of Portland. Part of Chesil Beach encloses a

Chesil Beach, Dorset, England, is a special type of spit called a tombolo—it links an island with the mainland.

long, narrow tidal lagoon called the Fleet. In time the Fleet, the Polish *haffs*, and all the lagoons trapped behind spits and bars will silt up and become marshlands.

Deltas

The Nile River in Egypt enters the Mediterranean Sea via a **delta**. Just north of Cairo, the Nile divides into two main channels. But there are a maze of smaller channels branching outward from these like the ribs of a fan. The land between all these watercourses is flat and low lying. It

has been built up by deposits carried by the Nile and dumped as the river entered the sea. These deposits are extremely fertile and the soils of the Nile delta have been cultivated by Egyptian farmers for centuries.

From the air the Nile delta looks like a fan roughly the shape of a triangle. The front of the delta bulges out into the Mediterranean like a great bow. This is because the delta is still being extended seaward.

Not all rivers have deltas. There are certain conditions necessary for a delta to develop. It is the rate of deposition that is most important. As a river enters the sea, its speed of flow is checked and it will deposit the material it is carrying. Where this is deposited faster than it can be removed by the sea, a delta develops. The deposits slowly build up until they stand above sea level and extend the land seaward. The mudflats of the delta surface cause the river to divide into many channels.

Not all deltas are of the characteristic

The Nile Delta in Egypt, photographed from a satellite circling the Earth.

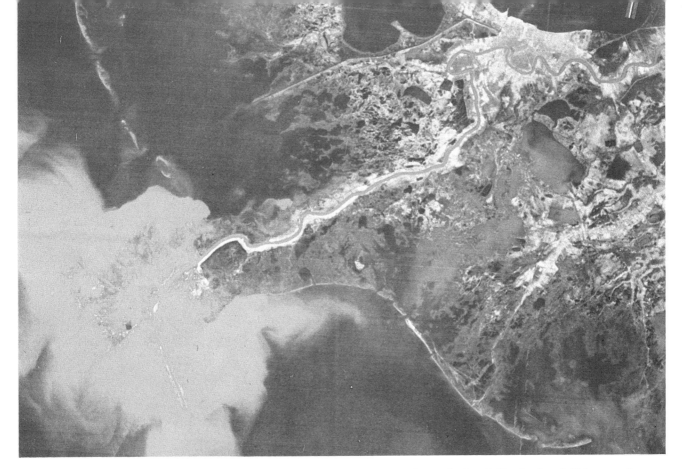

fan shape of the Nile, although the Rhône River in France and the Niger River in Nigeria both have fan-shaped deltas. The Mississippi River, in the U.S., has what is called a bird's-foot delta. Here the land is extending outward into the Gulf of Mexico in prongs, rather like the shape of a bird's foot. The Mississippi River is well known for the enormous amount of silt it

The delta of the Mississippi River; the pale blue 'cloud' on the left is silt being deposited where one channel of the river enters the Gulf of Mexico.

carries downstream—about 500 million tons each year—and the delta is growing rapidly.

Reclamation

In our modern overcrowded world, land is very valuable. It not only provides space for people to live and work, but also the place where food is grown and materials are mined for industry. These varied uses of the land often come into conflict with one another. There are sometimes arguments about whether farmland should be sold to build houses, or areas of forest cleared to make roads. Whatever decisions are reached, one thing is clear—land is too valuable for any of it to be lost.

This book has already shown how the sea erodes the land. You have read how fast erosion can take place on unprotected lowland coasts, especially where the rocks are soft and crumbly. Houses that were

Romney Marsh, Kent—one of the areas in Britain that have been reclaimed.

originally built inland now stand on the cliff edge, and will eventually collapse altogether. It is for this reason that so many coastlines are protected from the sea. Massive concrete sea walls have been built to protect stretches of coast that are particularly open to erosion. Unfortunately, not all the coast can be protected in this way. Sea defenses are difficult and expensive to build, and are themselves attacked by the sea and therefore often in need of repair.

In some places it is possible to make new land from the sea. This is done by reclamation. In many parts of Britain, former salt marshes have been reclaimed and are now being extensively cultivated. Romney Marsh in Kent, behind the great shingle ridge of Dungeness, has been reclaimed. So has much of the land around the Wash in East Anglia. In these marsh areas the first task is to drain off any saltwater. It is sometimes necessary to build a protective embankment around the area so that the sea cannot flood it again. Then the salt in the soil has to be "flushed out" by flooding the land with freshwater and draining this away. This may have to be done several times before the land is fit for cultivation.

New land is constantly being built up in deltas. The marshes that form here are reclaimed in a similar way to saltwater marshes, although it is usually not necessary to remove any saltwater. The wet marshlands of the Rhône and Mississippi deltas are used for rice growing.

The real experts at land reclamation are the Dutch. The Netherlands is a small country with a large population. For centuries the Dutch have had to build huge sea defenses called **dikes** to protect their land from flooding after violent North Sea storms. In the north of the country, a shallow bay called the Zuider Zee proved to be a great problem. To protect the land around the Zuider Zee, 360 kilometers (225 miles) of dikes were built. As the water was only 18 meters (60 feet) deep, and much of the seabed was made of clay, the Dutch decided to reclaim the Zuider Zee. The Great Dike was built across the mouth of the bay, and the saltwater was then drained out and replaced by freshwater to form the Ijssel Meer lake. Over the past 50 years, five huge areas of land called **polders** have been reclaimed. First, dikes were built,

Part of the Great Dike across the Ijssel Meer lake in the Netherlands.

and then the polders were drained. Pumping stations have to work all the time to keep the land dry by drawing water from the surface soil and draining it into canals.

Not only has the Zuider Zee plan successfully protected a large part of the Netherlands from flooding; it has also added 2,250 square kilometers (870 square miles) to the area of the country. The Dutch have similar plans to reclaim more of their coastal areas.

Changing levels of the sea

Erosion and deposition help to change the shape of the coast. But there are times when a coastline undergoes more major changes. Although the level of the land and sea appear to be stable, at times the height of the land in relation to the sea can change. This has occurred several times in the past.

A fall in the level of the land or a rise in the level of the sea produces a drowned or **submerged coastline**. Since the last ice age the sea level has risen considerably—perhaps as much as 120 meters (400 feet). This was caused by the melting of the vast icecaps. As the sea level has risen, it has drowned much of the former land surface. Totally different coastlines develop in drowned lowland areas and submerged upland areas.

Submerged lowland coasts

In the lowlands, a rise in sea level causes the sea to flood any low coastal areas and penetrate inland to drown the lower parts of river valleys. The sea also covers the flood plains to either side of the river. The lower river valley then becomes an **estuary**, a tidal arm of the sea. The old flood plains are often uncovered at low tide, revealing a complex of mudflats and creeks.

An estuary at low tide, with boats resting on the mudflats.

The old river course is marked by a deep-water channel running up the estuary, which allows ships to penetrate inland to sheltered waters. This is one reason why so many major port cities have developed on estuaries. London on the Thames estuary in England is an example. So is Hamburg on the Elbe in Germany, and New York on the Hudson in the United States. Unfortunately, when an estuary is formed, the river enters the sea much higher up its valley. Therefore the river deposits any material it is carrying in the estuary, which gradually silts up. For this reason, it is often necessary to dredge the deep-water channel to keep it open for shipping. This and the increase in the size of ships has led to the opening of **outports** farther downstream on many estuaries. In England, for example, Tilbury is about 35 kilometers (22 miles) downstream from London; in Germany, Bremerhaven is the outport for Bremen. Even so, the water in many of the estuarine ports is not deep enough to accommodate large modern oil tankers.

Although we are no longer in an ice age, the polar regions are still covered by vast ice caps. It has been estimated that if these

Opposite *Europoort is a new outport which has been built downstream from Rotterdam, in the Netherlands.*

ice caps melted, the sea level would rise by 70 meters (230 feet). This would be enough to flood many of the world's major ports and cities.

Flooding the uplands

When the ice caps melted at the end of the last ice age, so much water was released into the sea that even upland areas became submerged.

In the uplands, however, the flooding was not so broad as in the lowlands, but was limited to the river valleys. Tributary valleys were submerged as well as the main valley, producing deep-water branching inlets called **rias**, from which the land rises steeply on either side.

There are well-developed ria coastlines in southwest England, southwest Ireland, and northwest Spain. The deep water that exists in rias has been found to be very valuable—rias make excellent deep-water sites for oil tanker terminals.

During the last ice age, glaciers and ice caps covered much of the land. Some

glaciers carved valleys down to sea level. Once the ice had melted and the rising sea had drowned these valleys, **fjords** were formed. These are long, narrow inlets of the sea, sometimes with sharp bends and often reaching quite far inland. Norway has a spectacular fjord coastline. Indeed, Norway's coast is so indented that it is estimated if the fjords were straightened out, the coast would stretch halfway around the world. The longest fjord in Norway is the Sogne fjord. It is over 150 kilometers (90 miles) long, but no more

Fjords, like this one in Norway, are glacial valleys that were flooded when melting ice caused the sea level to rise after the last ice age.

than 5 kilometers (3 miles) across. Barren, rocky cliffs rise almost vertically from the water to a height of 1,600 meters (5,250 feet). As in all fjords, the water is deep—over 1,300 meters (4,265 feet) in places. But there is a sill or threshold near the entrance where the water shallows to about 100 meters (330 feet). The threshold marks the position of the terminal moraine. It is a ridge of pebbles, boulders and rubble deposited by the glacier when it melted.

There are also fjords along the west coast of Scotland where they are called sea lochs. Alaska, Chile and the southwest of South Island, New Zealand, also have fjord coastlines. Because of the magnificent scenery of the fjords, in all these countries the coast is a great tourist attraction.

The Dalmatian coast of Yugoslavia is another example of a submerged coast line. Originally, there were mountain chains running parallel to the coast, but when the sea level rose, these mountains became partially submerged. Some mountaintops now stand above the sea in the form of long, narrow islands.

The Dalmatian coast of Yugoslavia is a drowned upland coast; mountaintops now appear above sea level as islands.

During an ice age, the enormous weight of ice that builds up depresses the level of the land. When the ice melts, the land "bobs" up again.

36

Coasts that emerge from the sea

When the level of the land rises or the level of the sea falls, then an **emergent coastline** is formed. Emergent coastlines are less common than submerged coasts. A rise in the level of the land may be due to powerful movements within the Earth's crust, or they may be associated with glaciation. During the ice age, the amount of ice that builds up on the land is enormous. Its weight is sufficient to depress the level of the land. When the ice melts, the land "bobs" up again very slowly.

When a low-lying area is uplifted, a smooth coast with a gently shelving shore line results. Deposition, wave action and longshore drift build up offshore bars and spits with shallow lagoons behind. This type of coast can be found in southeastern United States and also in Sweden and Finland around the Gulf of Bothnia.

The emergence of an upland coast will lead to recutting of coastal features by the waves. The original beach and cliff line now stand above the level of a newly cut cliff and beach. If the uplift has been going on slowly over a long time there may be more than one **raised beach**, and the old cliff lines will stand well inland. There are raised beaches in New Zealand, Canada, Scandinavia, the United States, and on the coasts of north Wales and eastern Scotland. There are also raised beaches on many of the Scottish Islands—Arran, for example. These islands are generally rugged and bleak. The raised beaches, on the other hand, are level and often covered with fertile deposits. They provide some of the best farming land on these islands and are extensively cultivated. In these areas the raised beaches look like a series of steps.

A raised beach on the coast of Devon, in England. It is now well above sea level and can be used for cultivation.

Islands

There are tens of thousands of islands in the world, by no means all of them inhabited. Islands are not, of course, just isolated pieces of land floating in the sea; they are like the tops of mountains that rise up from the seafloor.

Continental and oceanic islands

Many islands, such as Tasmania, Newfoundland and the British Isles, are situated just offshore from a major land mass, and they rise from a shallow continental shelf. They are called **continental islands** and have the same rocks and structure as the nearby continent. Even their plant and animal life is very similar. In the past, such islands must have been joined to their neighboring continent. Their separation was probably due either to the strip of land between the islands and the mainland sinking, or to the rise in

Opposite *Tasmania, which is just offshore from Australia, is a continental island.*

sea level after the last ice age. Long ago, there must have been a "land bridge" across the Bering Strait between Asia and North America, since the Eskimos and American Indians are related to the Mongolian peoples of Central Asia. Their ancestors traveled across the land bridge before the sea level rose.

Some continental islands—New Zealand, for example—have very different plant and animal life from their nearest continent. They must, therefore, have been separated much longer ago to allow time for this to occur.

Islands that lie in the open ocean far away from any continent and rise out of deep water are called **oceanic islands**. These islands are indeed mountaintops. Earth movements sometimes push up great submarine ridges in the oceans, and oceanic islands are the summits of these ridges standing above sea level. The Azores, Ascension Island, and Tristan da Cunha all stand on the Mid-Atlantic Ridge.

Many oceanic islands are volcanic. When volcanoes erupt under the sea, they build up until they stand above the surface. The Hawaiian Islands are volcanic, and one of the volcanoes—

The Azores are situated in the middle of the Atlantic Ocean, a great distance from any continent; they are called oceanic islands.

Mauna Kea—is the tallest mountain in the world, rising to a height of 10,023 meters (33,476 feet) above the seafloor.

One strange feature of volcanic islands is that they can appear or disappear quite suddenly. The island of Surtsey appeared off the coast of Iceland in 1963, during a volcanic eruption. But when Krakatoa erupted in 1883, it exploded with such violence that most of the island was blown away.

Living islands

Corals exposed at low tide.

One group of oceanic islands are very special in the way they develop. These are the **coral islands**. Corals are very beautiful and are often brilliantly colored.

A coral is actually a colony of tiny animals. Each animal is called a polyp. It is rather like a sea anemone. The polyp forms a hard chalky cup around itself, like an outer skeleton. When the polyp has grown to a certain size, a "bud" appears on the side and grows into another polyp. This happens again and again. The polyps never separate, so they slowly evolve into colonies. As the polyps attach themselves to something solid, the colonies gradually build into large coral formations. It has been estimated that corals can grow 1.5 meters (5 feet) in a hundred years.

E 3105

Corals can only live in warm, shallow, clear water. The sea temperature must be above 20°C (68°F), and the water no deeper than 80 meters (260 feet). Because of the complicated way in which the polyps make their skeletons, they cannot survive in dirty or polluted water. Plenty of oxygen and plankton are also necessary to keep the polyps alive. These conditions only exist in certain parts of the tropics. The Bahamas, in the Caribbean Sea, are coral islands, but the Pacific Ocean has more coral formations than any other ocean. Indeed, part of the Pacific Ocean is called the Coral Sea.

There are four types of coral form-ations. Atolls are roughly circular in shape and surround a shallow lagoon. The Gilbert islands are atolls. Fringing reefs grow close inshore around many islands in the Pacific and the Caribbean. Barrier reefs, on the other hand, grow on the continental shelf much farther off shore. The Great Barrier Reef off the coast of Queensland, Australia, is almost 2,000 kilometers (1,250 miles) long. It lies between 30 and 160 kilometers (18-100 miles) offshore. Not all reefs reach above sea level, and submerged reefs are very dangerous to ships.

No one really knows how all these coral formations develop. One problem is that coral is found deeper than 80 meters (260 feet), although the polyps cannot live as deep as this. So the coral must originally have grown in shallower water. One idea is that all the formations are really stages in coral growth around a slowly sinking island. First a fringing reef develops, which becomes a barrier reef and eventually an atoll when the original island has completely submerged.

Heron Island on the Great Barrier Reef, off the coast of Queensland, Australia.

Opposite *The Pacific island of Moorea with its fringing reef.*

Facts and figures

The highest officially recorded wave was measured in the Pacific Ocean in February, 1933; it was 34 meters (112 feet) from crest to trough.

The greatest tidal range in the world occurs in the Bay of Fundy in Nova Scotia; the greatest recorded range was 16.3 meters (53.5 feet).

The highest tsunami was off Ishigaki Island in the Ryukyu Chain, Japan, on April 24, 1971; it was 85 meters (278 feet) high, and so powerful that it tossed a 750-ton block of coral more than 2.5 kilometers (1.5 miles).

The highest sea cliffs in the world are on the north coast of Molokai in the Hawaiian Islands; they are 1,005 meters (3,300 feet) high.

The largest bay in the world is Hudson Bay in northern Canada; it has a shoreline 12,268 kilo meters (7,623 miles) long, and an area of 822,300 square kilometers (317,500 square miles).

The longest fjord in the world is Nordvest Fjord in eastern Greenland; it is 313 kilometers (195 miles) long.

The world's longest estuary is that of the Ob in the USSR, which is 885 kilometers (550 miles) long.

The largest delta in the world is formed by the Ganges and the Brahmaputra in Bangladesh and West Bengal, India; it covers an area of 75,000 square kilometers (30,000 square miles).

The largest island in the world is Greenland, which has an area of 2,175,000 square kilo meters (840,000 square miles).

The newest island is Lateiki Island, Tonga, which appeared in June, 1979, after a volcanic eruption.

The world's largest coral atoll is Kwajalein in the Marshall Islands, in the Pacific Ocean; its reef encloses a lagoon of 2,850 square kilometers (1,100 square miles).

The longest coral reef is the Great Barrier Reef off northeastern Australia; it is 2,027 kilometers (1,260 miles) long.

Glossary

Backwash The movement of seawater down the beach after a wave has broken.

Bar A ridge of sand or shingle formed across a bay or mouth of a river. The sediment is deposited when the current carrying it is slowed down in some way.

Bayhead bar A bar that grows from one headland to another, across a bay.

Beach The strip of land bordering the sea, lying between the high and low water marks. It may be boulders, pebbles or sand.

Bedding plane The surface that separates one layer of rock from another.

Bench A platform cut by the waves at the foot of a cliff. Only the upper part of the platform is visible at low tide. The platform slopes gently seaward and disappears below the water.

Blowhole A vertical shaft connecting a sea cave with the surface above. During storms, spray is forced up through the blowhole from waves breaking in the cave below.

Coastal dunes Dunes formed on the coast by wind blowing across a wide, sandy beach.

Continental island An island situated just off shore from a large land mass.

Coral Colonies of tiny animals that form atolls, fringing reefs and barrier reefs.

Corrasive action The wearing away of rocks by pebbles and sand carried by waves.

Crest The top of a wave.

Delta New land that is gradually built up at the mouth of a river.

Deposition The dropping of the material carried by the sea when free movement of the water is interrupted in some way.

Dikes Sea defenses in the Netherlands.

Emergent coast A coast that is rising relative to sea level.

Erosion The gradual wearing away of the land by various natural forces, such as water, wind and ice. Water is mainly responsible for coastal erosion.

Estuary The funnel-shaped mouth of a river. Estuaries are tidal and are places where freshwater and seawater mix.

Fetch The length of open water over which the wind blows.

Fjord A long, narrow, steep-sided inlet of sea that penetrates an upland coast. Fjords were cut by glaciers and then flooded when the ice melted.

Geo A long, narrow tidal inlet cut into the cliff face. Geos probably developed from collapsed caves.

Hydraulic action The wearing away of rocks by waves trapping air in crevices in the cliff.

Lagoon A narrow stretch of water separated from the sea by a spit, bar, or coral reef.

Longshore drift The movement of material along the coast.

Neap tides Tides that have the least range, i.e. when the difference between high tide and low tide is smallest. They occur when the sun and the moon are at right angles to each other and thus pull the Earth's oceans in different directions.

Oceanic island   An island in the open ocean, far from any large land masses.

Outport   A port built downstream from a main estuary port.

Polder   An area of reclaimed land in the Netherlands.

Raised beach   A beach raised by earth movements, often with inland cliffs behind.

Ria   A long, narrow (often branching) inlet of sea, formed by the drowning of a river-valley system in an upland coastal area.

Saltation   The movement of small particles of sediment by waves and currents.

Sea loch   A fjord in Scotland.

Shingle   Coarse, seashore gravel.

Solvent action   The wearing away of rocks by chemicals dissolved in sea water.

Spit   A feature similar to a bar, except one end is joined to the land.

Spring tides   Tides that have the greatest range, i.e. when the difference between high tide and low tide is greatest. They occur when the sun and the moon are in line with the Earth, and are thus exerting the maximum pull on the oceans.

Stack   A rocky pillar near the coast, left by the erosion of a headland.

Submerged coast   A coast that has fallen relative to sea level.

Swash   The movement of seawater up the beach after the breaking of a wave.

Tombolo   A bar or spit connecting a pre-existing island to the mainland.

Transportation   The movement of eroded material by waves and currents.

Trough   The lowest point in a wave.

Tsunami   A large sea wave caused by an earthquake or volcanic eruption below the seabed.

Further reading

Angel, Heather. *Life on the Seashore.* Morristown, NJ: Silver Burdett, 1979.

Bendick, Jeanne. *Exploring an Ocean Tide Pool.* Westport, CT: Garrard Publishing, 1976.

Braun, Earnest and Brown, Vinson. *Exploring Pacific Coast Tide Pools.* Happy Camp, CA: Naturegraph, 1966.

Leonard, Jonathan. *Atlantic Beaches.* Morristown, NJ: Silver Burdett, 1972.

Life at the Seashore. Washington, D.C.: National Geographic Society, 1981.

Maidoff, Ilka. *Let's Explore the Shore.* New York: Astor-Honor, 1962.

Stephens, William. *Life in the Tidepool.* New York: McGraw-Hill, 1975.

Zim, Herbert S. *Waves.* New York: William Morrow, 1967.

Index

Picture acknowledgements

The illustrations in this book were supplied by: Mark Boulton 22, Jane Burton 7, Eric Crichton 5, 10, 14, Adrian Davies 13, Nicholas Devore 43, Geoff Dore 24, Jennifer Fry 37, Arnold Kidson 25, 31, M. Timothy O'Keefe 41, Fritz Prenzel 38, Bill Wood 42—all from Bruce Coleman; Biofotos 17; Bill Donohoe 36; Geoscience Features 9, 11, 19, 20, 21, 28; Geoslides 34, 35; Netherlands National Tourist Office 30; Photo Research International *front cover*, 16, 23, 26, 27; Portuguese National Tourist Office 40; Malcolm S. Walker 6, 18; Zefa 15, 33. The remaining pictures are from the Wayland Picture Library.